Interrogation Room

T0160514

Interrogation Room

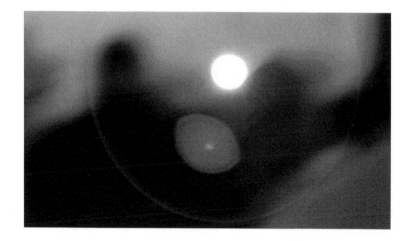

Jennifer Kwon Dobbs

WHITE PINE PRESS / BUFFALO, NEW YORK

White Pine Press
P.O. Box 236 Buffalo, NY 14201
www.whitepine.org

All rights reserved. This work, or portions thereof, may not be reproduced in any form without the written permission of the publisher.

Copyright © 2018 Jennifer Kwon Dobbs

Publication of this book was made possible, in part, by public funds from the New York State Council on the Arts, a State Agency; and with funds from the National Endowment for the Arts, which believes that a great nation deserves great art.

Cover Art: *Dorason May 24, 2015.* Digital C-print, Jane Jin Kaisen, 2015.

Printed and bound in the United States of America.

Library of Congress Control Number: 2017946297

ISBN 978-1-945680-15-1

Interrogation Room

CONTENTS

///

for Omma and Appa

and all of our missing relations
in northern and southern Korea
east and west

Article 7: Praise, Encouragement, Etc.
(I) Any person who, with the knowledge that such action threatens the nations existence and security and the order of liberal democracy, praises, encourages, advertises or supports the activities of an Anti-state Organization or its members, or advertises or advocates a rebellion against the State shall be punishable by imprisonment for a term of not exceeding 7 years.

Article 10: Failure to Report
Any person who, possessing knowledge of a person who has committed one of the crimes as set forth in Articles 3 and 4, and Sections (I) and (3) of Article 5, has failed to report the matter to an investigation or intelligence authority, shall be punishable by imprisonment of a term of not exceeding 5 years or a fine not exceeding two million Won. Provided, however, that if the above-mentioned person has a family relationship with the offender of the stipulated crime, the punishment hereunder may be either mitigated or remitted.

— National Security Law, Republic of Korea

I confess I traveled █████████████. I confess I
███████ northward in Korea searching ██████
███████. I confess I traveled northward in Korea
searching my face, rewiring my mouth to sing █████
████████████████ My mouth searched my face,
traveling northward for Korea. I confess I
rewired in order to sing as one. We are ████████
because we come from a mother. Please do not
search my mother who doesn't know. I confess for
we. Searching the wiring, the Korea inside my
mouth, northward, face, please, my name is ██████

to North Korea … traveled | Seodaemun Prison, Seoul 1919

Here are notes rolled into plugs. Tongue them into the ears of twelve who will arrange outside a letter of independence. Fragment to prevent police capture then disperse among the singing: Americans admired the Japanese imperialist machine as the East's sole hope for modernity, especially the panopticon that administered a colonial body open to the warden's gaze. Wings graft a soul where before rooting and suckling. Inside solitary, mother every life known since descending breech. Multiply selves as a refusal to sign a conversion statement. Brother silence, pale sister whose gray hair petals in wait for love's return.

~~for my mother~~ | Saddleback Church, Lake Forest 2012

Insert children into crates. Unswaddle to receive the singing. Unto Him take the youngest girls into lace aprons, boys into seersucker suits. Take parts the ancestors lick to identify the taste. (Yes—a child easily sheds grammar.) Don't take to save. Suffer only the innocents among the Fatherless to raise in His image for whomsoever takes the orphan first He shall control past and future.

~~Uri Hana/We are one … one Korea~~ | Battleship Island 1930

Take young men as coal miners, young women as comfort because
Confucian virgins. Take copper, bauxite, tungsten, gold out of the
dead's rosaries. Take hair for rope to hoist up station shafts then cross
off weekly checklists. Take underground schoolteachers who refuse to
give names. Into conscription take their sons / daughters shall take a
daily quota of soldiers to maintain the front's health.

The Origins Inside Kim Dae Shik

Manchukuo 1938 | Director of Holt Adoption Agency, Seoul 1979-1981

Scrape the southern regime's continuous present. There is a forgetting

        He photographed me draped in a yukata of chrysanthemums

enforced by scorched earth raids, a burning cow charging the house

       yellow sycamore and red oak leaves. It was autumn in Pittsburgh.

again, again its pink mouth opening like a fist letting go of time.

       He was an artist; I was a poet. Transracially adopted, we made love

The image replays in a survivor's sleep, a Japanese officer's blueprint

       inside our Korean names—Kwon Young Mee, Kim Dae Shik.

for tactical teams trained in Manchukuo to terrorize the guerillas' wives

       We plundered our bodies' fragrance so exotic were we to each other

kidnap their children—industry of sympathy to rehabilitate the patriots

       that, as I mounted his hips, I was his sister, mother, aunt, and child

shamed, their hands moving the conveyer belt of extracted ore

       fastened to him like parasitic limbs striking his chest for meat

to build the state. The orphan master extends his name to each male.

A Forest in Jeju, Southern Korea

for Jane Jin Kaisen

Crows caw
in slow motion

shroud the ancestor
trees. A boy

piles brown leaves
out of range

as Jane's camera follows
the murder

dissecting. It's 1948
after a scorched earth raid.

He hides under brown
improvised

from neighbors' corpses,
conceals

his baby sister inside
a cow's gutted stomach.

Impassive
a U.S. Army truck locks

a panoramic shot
captioned "a cleansing."

Gangsters scatter
cobalt fire while

the *Stars and Stripes*
stands by directing

scenery, so much
scenery, so much crying out

edited out,
muted, painted red.

He escaped
the frame, and in Jane's film

he survives
disembodied, all breath

like walking
with handfuls of dry leaves

to cover that fetid scent
enticing

a darkness.
It whirls in to snatch

the choicest parts
scalped, hair still attached

in patches. It's 2011
when Jane films.

His voice circles
my imperfect translation:

a winged cloud
unlaced a face

from bone, grafted
tongue to bark

for intricate nests,
tinkered with brown.

I wanted to save
each one I could name—

손가락, 눈, 이
fingers, eyes, teeth—

but there were too many,
too many birds building.

Northern Korea Postcard

Downtown Pyeongyang

What you're encouraged to see—avenues meticulously swept,

white magnolias lacing the Taedong River's edge—

does not repair your divided heart or the darkness

news wires have trained your eyes to search out, to contort

grandmothers who stretch in those trees' shade into shades.

Through the tour van's windows, you look for rage,

and outrage installs black mirrors in skyscrapers

you're convinced stand empty. Uncles squat to play yutnori,

and they're orphans tossing hollow bones. Why

when a truck blares songs to urge the masses to struggle

for national prosperity, do you curse every tan stranger

to a birdcage hunger and a dictator's heel? Why

when a red-scarfed boy waves do you avert your gaze,

and the van's glass frame splits your reflection?

Northern Korea Postcard

International Friendship Exhibition

You want to throttle the wax statue of Kim Il Sung,

his plastic deer, blue thrushes. Shrubs hide

industrial fans whirring to preserve

the people's gift sprayed to resemble flesh.

Instead you bow. Foreigner you lay wreaths,

bouquets, and praise at the Great Leader

and Dear Leader's bronze feet. What do you seek

as you gain greater access to the interior

of your disgust dressed in shorts and flip flops

and where no light or dust is allowed?

Northern Korea Postcard

Myohyangsan National Forest

For beauty you must forget yourself

and give in when your guide Ms. Han

takes your hand so you both can walk

on slippery stones to a boulder under maples,

the mountain river rushing beyond time

where two girls cross. Their white hanbok hems

drink the cool water, and their bare feet test

footholds. Each sister trusts the way her sister

steadies her step before they move on

Northern Korea Postcard

Driving in South Hwanghae Province

While Professor Jeong explains a poet

should work with farmers to write of harvest,

you recall 160 kilometers away Professor Kim

said there's no poetry in the north.

Both answers seem compelled by law

concealing a revolver aimed at the senses

alert to an intruding thought. What of you

who dwells at the border

adopted by all four directions

the grass recovers as its own? It roots

in landmines, seeds ghosts who owe allegiance

only to where they're buried. You're

a fleeting image to these cornfields

that don't know you

were forcibly removed from the south,

that transgress the border

like a tunneling army turns and overturns

every stone to unlock forbidden ground

Northern Korea Postcard

Panmunjom, DMZ | for Caitlin Kee

Tourists on the southern side strain

to take shots of a real NK soldier

who led you to this balcony. *Don't cry,*

she said on the stairs. *They win*

when they see you cry. So you gaze

at a plank that marks the center

between northern and southern Korea.

You study the wood's pale grain,

its slightly skewed position due to time,

and you guess its weight, how many

winters it lay there in the sand

a witness to the same spectacle

patrol its length. You measure how far

from your mother's house in Daegu

to your father's house in Seoul

to your hotel in Pyeongyang

near the Ministry of Commerce to prove

the intimate distances that bind

your heart here to the young woman's

stoicism and the proud southern youth

who could be your cousin

trained as a sharpshooter

to avoid eye contact. You turn away

from the gawking SK tour guide's

binoculars, the bused Greeks

thrilled by their glimpse of two NK women

they assume are somber due to hunger,

and you remember the great poet Kim So Wol

was a northerner born in Pyeonganbuk-do:

When seeing me sickens you,

I'll not struggle. I'll gather

armfuls of azaleas from a southern mountain

and scatter them on your path

Reading Keith Wilson's "The Girl"

Yes, I've thought about tone
how white space stages

Korea 1953.
A girl silk-gowned,
small breasts, thin
indirect face.

Whether
Wilson carved away

the naval officers'
crisp white kits
in an Incheon officers club

himself a young sailor
curious, a boy

slung to the right.
Pinched and swollen

the hand-rolled joints dangled
between the men's thighs

as they fingered and flicked
hot off each other
and at last, *in the dark,*

Wilson
the lips parted
swallowed the cherry.

& how easily [he] came
marks of rank about him
so delicious

that later
in passion
in light not understood

he scratched out
the foreign words
coaxed from the men's creased hems,

and for *the crinkle of paper*
passing hands, he wrote "The Girl."

It had to be a girl.

Birthfather

Camp Long, Gangwon-do, Southern Korea

Here I am unmothered and unfathered
yet born of a mother and father

rumored to have screwed in a basement bar
now a DVD room you can rent per hour,

faux leather couches, Coca Cola, 24-hour action
flicks where you're Indiana Jones or an astronaut

cowboy who always gets the girl. That girl
haunts as I descend each metal step

into the graffiti throat of their past
that might've been boot sludge, orange stain,

some trace of a G.I. shaking his cock
to wake up, his knuckled hardness

hungry for a rouged face. He is giver and taker
paying the permed mamasan who guards the door,

the clock, her girls, and now my father
who slips through bead curtains, sheets, lace, lips.

I can't go down as he went down cocksure
she wanted this. I pull back. I look away. I can't

say he knelt in shame or covered her eyes
fixed on ceiling cracks to divide herself. I can't

deny I want them here fucking against time. I can't
say otherwise when the ajossi grabs my arm

and mistakes me for someone else: a Korean woman
blocking the stairwell and forgetting herself.

This—

Master Sergeant B | Korea 195? and Northfield 2009

I too want to forget the image
        properly buried in the Gangwon forest
                reclaimed by grass

I tire of all this seeing
        that's not seeing a head turning
                on a rifle's mouth

turning puss-swollen
        eyes chapped by wind
                rustling mountain trees

the soldier's red hair
        As he raises his rifle toward the trees
                the head spins

in four directions
        shock the birds hear. The birds
                scatter

and arch their dark backs
        A cry snaps through their necks
                as they lift up

as one to the sky
        faraway from the forest while
                the soldier stares

into the sun's black eye
> he can still describe as an old professor
>> He smiles

at that distance
> His hands again cradle the rifle's head
>> in the photograph

he'll pass around
> the lecture hall for his students to see
>> what he remembers

of mud, the enemy, thirst, this—
> no one can identify or bring home
>> to bury

This is his image
> the birds can't read and can't forget
>> a ricochet

wind from the sun
> a wind driving them from that tree
>> flared

in the sun's center
> like an unshuttered lens. Time captures
>> his hands

his regalia pose
> exposed to a light that rends apart
>> like this—

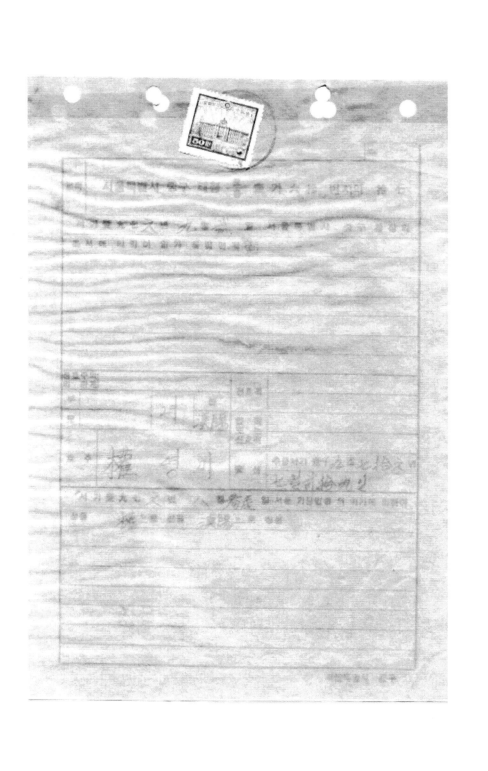

Notes from a Missing Person

To search for Mother's body is to listen with a poet's attention that can rub across the word's surfaces for a pulse. Mother, you sit across from a social worker—a woman who is your same age—flipping through pages and indicating where you should sign. You're pregnant—heavy with me during your sixth month—leaning slightly backward because your lower back aches. The social worker—maybe a mother, herself—disassociates from the fact that your bodies, sitting so close to each other, can do the same work: Your pen following the social worker's finger to where you should leave your mark.

Your bodies are so close to each other that they become one body linked through paper—one that gives and one that takes away. Above you, Jesus points to his thorn-crowned heart and looks beyond the frame's plastic edge. On the social worker's desk, a wedding photo and a little boy laughing and running toward the camera. His right hand holds a red-stitched baseball. The social worker, anxious to return home, checks the paperwork and clips it inside a brown folder marked with a case number. She puts her hand on your shoulder to reassure you. You lean against a mother who wants to rush home to her child in Samsong-dong and who doesn't see you as a mother. You blur together—one taking/one giving me away.

What proof do I have that this is your story? I can only see the space. Here's a round black table, a set of gray office chairs upholstered in the Danish functional style. Here's a tissue box, a beige telephone with a red button to place a call on hold. Here are the fluorescent lights. I can hear typing next door. White industrial linoleum flecked with multi-colored chips doesn't muffle noise. Color portraits of joyful adoptive parents show mothers what they can't provide. Tan metal file cabinets. A water cooler dispenses hot and cold. Maxim coffee sticks, styrofoam cups, English tea.

I can see the conversations around this table, the frayed gray fabric, split orange foam, the cooler's cloudy plastic, and water damage stains on the ceiling because the building was hastily constructed (as were all offices during the 70s). You would've been childbearing age—anywhere from 18 to 45—and capable of working in one of many light industrial factories constructed during Park Chung Hee's regime when South Korea engineered its economic miracle on your back leaning over a steady conveyer belt of t-shirts, tennis shoes, toys, tooth brushes, combs, and plastic mirrors crated for export. Your hands rush to keep up with the manufacturing speedway toward South Korea's revolution from an agriculture-based nation to an economic tiger. You're a farmer's daughter from Jeolla-do or Gangwon-do or maybe one of Seoul's own wanting to earn some money for family back home still squatting in an unheated room to shower with a hose. So when the social worker asks if you would sign here, you watch your hand move knowing that you will say nothing to your father or mother who take the money to buy food and encourage you to eat well.

You eat in silence that night. You feed us both with your grief.

What am I saying? I can only describe a researched context, a slanted shadow. I can only speculate and dramatize because I can't find you. Is this a fetish or a document of desire? This is not your body. This is not mine. This is my tongue—meat flapping inside my crushed mouth. The military meat that Korea imports from the U.S.—spam/variety meats/mad cow/neo-liberal trade—ends up in budae jigae, a stew of scraps.

_____ 님이 가족찾기 하고 있는 중인데 혹시 (입양) 서류를 볼 수 있을까요?

_____ 님이 가족찾기 하고 있는 중이라 자기 서류를 보고 싶은데 갖고 있나요?

Can we see _____ documents? Do you have ___ documents? I don't want constellations.

Which story is mine? Which story is yours?

My documents are yours, aren't they? The words that took me from you had to admit first that I belonged to you—that you're woman's flesh, not a social artifact—even as they erased your name. I don't know your name. I only know this body that came from yours. I only know this page. I try to rewrite this language that took my body away from your body knowing that I will only clear this page of fetishes you would never use for yourself—birth mother, gift giver, social artifact, dead memory, trace, smear, signature, ____, n/a, unknown, even mother. No, Omoni, you wouldn't have dressed like these, and if I push through your skirts, I find blankness, this smoothness that is not your face.

███████████████

Birth mother, gift giver, social artifact, dead memory, trace, smear, signature, ____, n/a, unknown, even mother. What is the point of calling you such names and pronouncing you a lost or separated part, if not to drain our bodies of blood?

We do not stand across the DMZ at Panmunjom bused in for goodwill sunshine—lucky ticket holders drawn from the lottery mass of halmanideul and harabojideul who are desperate to see their parents before either one of them dies. To die with some relief, that is not our cause although we're also fighting time. I'm 33 years old and still able to bear a child, your grandchild. Can I even speak for you when it comes to our separation, your distance from those who sleep in my body? I can only talk around you overlapping myself. Don't daughters do this when they talk about their mothers?

When my mom was pregnant with me, she didn't have nausea.

My mother's bone marrow matched mine.

It's funny how we both worry about details! Just the other day, mom called—

I see your face—the flicker of you as I have come to know you—in the mothers at Ae Ran Won, the mothers who are heavy and tired walking up the stairwells of Dong Bang. In the footage reels that I have watched of Achim Madang, I have witnessed mothers grabbing grown men and pressing their foreheads to their necks—women half the height of the men—and holding their sons with a fierceness that can't be love. The television host interrupts to try to get the mother to separate for the interview. The camera circles to zoom in for the mother's eyes, the man's eyes who do not recognize this woman who is his mother stroking his face and refusing to share this moment for which she has hungered. The camera tightens the shot to document the mother locking her son's face against her chest perhaps in protection. Music. Clapping. Strangers watch, entertained.

Commercial break: 처음 처럼

Sitting around a red plastic table, four students shoot Chamisul soju. Hongdae pulses and basses in the background. It's their first time, and they're living it up!

The brown-haired girl in a pale Burberry top will actually fall in love.

How is hope—this blood call—used against us?

What is the difference between this television show and this smear on the page, Omoni? Both of them shame us, yes? Yet you can't read this page, can you? I'm torn from your gaze. What kind of freedom is this not to be able to ask if you're hungry? Or not to ask at all and set down a plate of cut pears that you can find after a good sleep?

▬▬▬▬▬▬▬▬▬▬

Omoni, they forced your mind to desert your body—your child to desert your body—and that removal someone else called an act of love. Yet love does not give life away. It gives life a way. It gives, and it gives. Your mind accepted your body as a vacancy, verdant yet razed to clear a way that no one celebrated or wept for. Did they know of your body emptied and discharged from the hospital, your breasts aching with milk to nourish your child, your back carrying your child to the orphanage, or your legs folded underneath your body bent forward in shame? Did they know how good your body was to deliver such a healthy child? (Receiving nations praise Korea for its perfect, beautiful infants.) Did they know of your body ruptured and stitched lying in the hospital bed connected to a monitor? Your body, stretch-marked and sagging where life had grown (where I had grown), climbs Dobongsan, Bukhansan, or Gwanaksan to see this vacancy inside you cupping Seoul bulldozing itself to rebuild as quickly as possible, straining against three mountains. Neon spills, honks, drinks, and advertises global progress:

43

Learn English! Harvard English Institute. The English Language Academy. English Now! These words whirl, grinding against your arms and face, while across the ocean, someone is holding your child, crying in happiness in a language that your child is scared of. Learn forgetfulness: Someone is lighting a candle a year later for your child's adoption day. Your child is laughing. Someone is telling your child that you gave him away because you loved him so much. And you become a "birth mother" who someone says loved so deeply that you gave him to her to love.

███████████████

Even in the act of deconstruction, there's a violence that siphons from your body, which my friend Kit Myers says is "the always becoming sign of 'family' that is instituted by the trace." Even in the word "family" there's your specter breathing through. This slashing away from your signifying body—on your body—constitutes Frederic Jameson's radical break "with another moment of socioeconomic organization and cultural and aesthetic orientation. [Your body] is defined against what it is not, against conditions which no longer prevail or are somehow irrelevant." What is irrelevant, Omoni, and what is not? Who decides context? Who empties the sign draining it of reproductive power rerouted to power some overseas simulacrum?

Disney World. It's a small world after all?

It's a beautiful child. It's not your child.

███████████████

Omoni, I was never as strong as you. I was 25 years old in love with a young man who wanted your grandchild but feared providing for him. We were both students. We were poor and young. We named it Juan Alejandro. Él era tres meses en mi matriz. I know because—as I laid on my back while the nurse slathered jelly on my stomach and rubbed a paddle across it for the ultrasound—the masked doctor pulled off his gloves sighing, "I don't think I got it all," and I thought of you letting go of me in the orphanage/shelter/hospital/alley/bedroom. I thought of you lying on your back, your legs spread, and your young body cold on a flat surface.

I was your body struggling with possibility. Thighs parted and feet in stirrups, I opened wide for instruments. "No, there's still more. See," said the nurse while AM radio played. She swiveled the monitor toward the doctor who squinted at the green pixels pulsing in the black screen. He untied his mask and took a break. The nurse put down the paddle and walked after him. I lied on the table with that vacancy I had chosen. Its trace—green static in void—still moved in my body, and I felt that darkness as separation from you, me, him. The three of us lied there together connected by our bodies lost to emptiness only a woman's body can suffer for the three of us. Loss skinned and bound us across three generations.

———

He came back, strapped on his mask, and leaned in siphoning. I wanted him to stop, but I was afraid. I couldn't say no. I said no. I said yes. I couldn't change my mind. I wanted to change my mind. I couldn't stop the machinery, couldn't stop the procedure for which I paid, Omoni.

You never gave money. No one paid you. In Korea, they pay bad women who derail economic progress with shame, not cash. Maybe you were a student, a divorcé with runs in her stockings, an irregular worker punching keys to ring up blue sponges, or a migrant stripping off plastic gloves after the assembly line belt whirrs to a stop. Maybe you were a teenager cramming for a chemistry exam or walking arm and arm with your girlfriends passing Yongsan's kijichon where the yuribang women lean against glass. Their pink glittery lips pressing hot O, pale arms and legs spreading X.

You definitely were because you gave me life; yet you lie beyond narration though others like to conceptualize you as averted damage, the what-could've-been-had-we-not-chosen-to-adopt, incapable child birthing a helpless child. I was saved from your body. Assimilation begins by fearing your body — my Korean woman's body — by carving trauma on it, a talk-story rerouting our roots toward confusion and shame. Who has the right to imagine your body away from my body? It's not your body, I fear, but this imagination saying to me before I learned how to read:

"You know what a martini is?" says a lieutenant from Akron, Ohio.

"Shaken," my mother giggles, swinging her legs. "No stir."

The lieutenant pinches my mother on the cheek and puts his arm around her. Later that night after last call, he pushes a $10 bill into her hand and licks her ear.

"Stir is better. Let's go."

Mother giggles, rolls the bill up, and then slides it into her shoe.

━━━━━━━━━━

What is this reality that's always a phantom that's neither an absence nor presence, neither flesh nor shadow? It's a fiction that haunts where the body should've been, a story that strikes out for a body with memory's force.

"Where are you from?" asks my best friend's sister, the basketball team's homecoming queen. She sits down on the den's shag floor and opens her French manicure set.

"My mother's from Korea, and my father is an American soldier," I say.

"Really?" My best friend's sister shakes a jar of angel kiss and applies a thin coat in two thick strokes on her left thumbnail.

"I'm a bastard," I say, trying to copy her technique with Blue #52 on my best friend's toes.

She continues to paint. "That's not true. Only boys can be bastards."

"Korean girls can be bastards." I slide the brush against the bottle's edge.

"Whatever," she says. "That's not Katie's color."

Another attempt.

Surrounded by sons, Mother is dying of cancer and asking for a daughter who she could not afford to keep. Her eldest son holds her hand. She describes walking up the hill to the orphanage's gate, the wet grass and mud, a dull ache in her shoulder as she searched for dry ground on which to set her child down, and her child waking up crying as if she knew that Mother was leaving her in the best way Mother knew how.

Switch off the cameras / Burn the scripts / Unplug / Blackout

What are these stories except tight shot reiterations looping with fresh props, wheeled-in sets, makeup, and redesigned lighting? A dubbed voice chases after a flamingo. What of the players who peel off your face—almond skin floating in saline solution, holes where breath and sight pierce through? Towels stained with flesh-colored cream, eyelashes dropped in a wastebasket—all these are a technology of story re-inventing and re-inventing. No wonder the Material Girl adopted twice from Malawi, though the second time she fought a higher court to overturn child protection laws so that she could take Chifundo away from her father James Kambewa, a domestic worker living in Blantyre, who learned from the media blitz that his daughter was alive.

███████████████

"This 1.1 birth rate is our revenge," says Ji-Young, "because we're treated so badly."

███████████████

At Duri Home, Omoni, you're taught to ritualize loss by sewing selvages and pleating skirts for first birthday clothes to accompany your baby overseas. This is not a gift to the adopters. It's your gift to your child so that she will remember you. I asked the mothers, and that's what they said about their labor. This body, this child of work belongs to you. It's a struggle to own what is yours beyond, as Hagen Koo says, "the dominant image of Asian female factory workers," which "is one of docility, passivity, transitory commitment to industrial work, and lack of interest in union activism." You're imagined as filial daughters/filial workers measuring blue cloth for hanbok: "Young female workers in the export sector" who are "controlled not only by the capitalist system but also by the patriarchal culture that had been reproduced in the industrial organization." Young women lean over gray Singer sewing machines pumping trundles with their left feet, feed red pant legs under the presser foot. This is also a language—love shows in details—measuring trim, hemming jackets for crisp collars and green sleeves. The rusted bobbin catches, and you pause to rethread, licking the edge to spear through the needle's eye. You whisper to the other omonideul that you're tired. (They've heard this before.) You can't work much longer. (They've heard this before.) Loss is a labor that's taking your child. The omonideul pause, listening.

Omonideul, what if you stood up like you did at Dongil Y.H. Company on July 25th with only your bodies against the dark blue uniforms and full riot gear? What if you link arms together to form a line between women carrying briefcases and your babies lying in plastic crates? What if before such violence, you remove your clothes and begin singing, your bodies swaying back and forth, salt and sweat, hair and wrinkles, your legs and arms wrapped together as one large embrace? To take your babies is to lay hands on your bodies and to pull apart your singing. What if you refuse to work and so force the dark uniforms to manhandle your bodies to show the violence that they ask you to do to yourselves?

███████████████

They use your love against you to take your children. As one omoni said to me, "They tell us we aren't good enough to raise our children. We can't provide them with private English lessons. How will our children grow up to succeed?"

███████████████

Omoni arm / 어머니의 팔 / Omoni legs / 어머니의 다리 / Omoni wrists / 어머니의 손목 / Omoni palms and shoulders / 어머니의 손바닥과 어깨뼈 / Omoni back and waist / 어머니의 등과 허리 / Omoni thumb, cheek, ears, and breasts / 어머니의 엄지 손가락, 볼, 귀와 가슴 / Omoni hipbone, eyes, and neck / 어머니의 관골, 눈과 목 / Omoni feet / 어머니의 발 / Omoni lips / 어머니의 입술

Your name is Shin Sun Mee, Lee Eun Hae, Kim Ok Shim, Kwon Joo Ae.

Your name is Truth, Beauty, Goodness, Grace, and Hopeful Justice.

I can recite your name's shape, which is not your name or its context.

I can listen around, above, and below it to draw an outline to hold in my mouth.

Is this a word—sand sliding through a sieve?

Is this your body—sand assuming a vase's shape?

A mother's fate is in her child's body.

As her child matures, a mother ages.

Sand pours from one glass to another to measure an hour.

One empties while another contains more possibility.

A body emerges from another, so a body may emerge from it.

A body gives, so another may give.

This is how narrative works: Time organized by causality's inner logic. Yet we were torn from one another, Omoni. I hear scraping whenever I say what's not your name.

I hear tanks rumble when I mispronounce Korean. I hear strafing when my eyes stop and fall mid-sentence, shocked and unable to get up. I see your mud-caked hand cover my hand as I steady the Korean language book. Your face coughs in the mirror as I attempt to mimic the shape: 어머니의 입술 grimaces, sucks in breath, and looks away.

If you were dead, I would know what to do: Lay out a chesa table with soju, fruit, and rice cakes. Stay up for three days drinking and singing with relatives. Make sure you never go hungry. Make sure you don't wander begging strangers for food.

Who are these strangers who tell me I have no right to my omoni's body? These unashamed strangers who know their mothers'

49

names and begrudge me mine?

Omoni, are you allowed to imagine me, or must you also turn to context out of need? Perhaps all you're allowed is me so that fear limits context—the day I was born, the memory of my body sliding out of yours, pink scars and lines my body wrote on yours that time fades? What sections of your memory do guards preside over, holding a nickel flashlight and a set of keys, opening bins and tossing files? The rattling in your head warns. I hear it too in the slow churn of helicopters preparing to take off, telephone line to headquarters crackling, underground drills boring for passageways that infantry could march through, police stacking shields for bus transport, basement pipes knocking while an ajossi buckles yet refuses to provide intelligence, the KCIA applying techniques learned from the CIA to compel an alleged traitor's conversion, a Parker pen drops on to tile, a map shudders, an omoni begs her eldest 아들 to confess because she and his younger brother are hungry, their stomachs knock and quiver, batons bang against bars to wake inmates who have been imprisoned on suspicion, and we're not supposed to know this, are we?

We're not supposed to recognize each another as family, yet this identification is embedded in our language. When we call out to strangers—unni, nuna, ajossi, halmoni and haraboji, we're one family/one Korea despite distance, difference in blood ties, and destruction of geographies and names. They say 네 in recognition, continuing their work without pause. An ajossi hands me change as I gather my bags and leave his cab. An unni nods toward where the napkins are, her fingers rolling kimbap and dotting the kim with water.

Omoni, what of the ruptured intimacy between us? What paper has disfigured our language such that we're unable to summon each other with our proper names? How must I break English so that you may recognize me? What parallel latitude cuts across our imaginations beginning with our bodies and what we can embody? If I never know your name, I will at least know the name that as your daughter

I should call you —엄마, not mother, not my mother—because I have learned this name for myself. I am 이라 딸, not somebody's daughter nor a gift that someone gave away.

To know this name is to embody relationships from which I have been estranged, to deregulate loves that I've been prevented from knowing and inheriting. This is another name for adoption if I look for bodies connected through your body, 엄마, which cluster together in my limbs, hair, nails and teeth, my ip and ko. This mouth is wae-haraboji. This nose is jin-halmoni. These eyes are yours. This forehead is samchon. These ears are shared by nam dongsaeng and unni. These words are our silences and speak only for me, and yet on this page, I can press my body to the ground in five directions with my body as the center. I can reach across distances that nations insist border us from each other. I can embrace you in forms that no one has imagined before or said because of shame. Hear this rattle? It's the call of bones to bones, muscles and tendons thrumming, the work of intestines and liver purifying the words to their elements to carry our singing across time and space. It's our most intimate speech.

우리 엄마 아게

미안해요. 나는 ~~실반했습습니다~~ 실패했습니다.
나는 아기 처럼 말해요. 피하지 않고 언어에서

배고퍼?

많이 먹어.

보고 싶어.

우리는 내변형 한국어 안에 갇혀 있다. 또 다시
반복해요.

어떻게 이 언어를 봉합할 수 있습니까?

그래서 우리는 서로를 찾을 수 있습니까?

우리는 어떻게 서로를 용서 할 수 있습니 까?
여기에서 우리는 항상 사과, 고기, 밥 과 물
압니다.

사랑해!

엄마 딸 수긴

Parasitic Twin

on a sculpture by Dana Weiser

The headless blue / torsos compete for care

Conjoined / the northern one drains nourishment

from the southern one / lithe and ambitious

all grand gestures / Each imitates the other to exceed the other

in a race of arms / of legs extended / the south extended

curves the white riser in salute / Its thin left calf strains

to stake more space / The north's left foot placed

flat hard to see how / from an aerial distance

What about the hands / for whom / do they reach?

Behold your miraculous body—decapitated, all affect

          Catherine, Sujin, Young Mee, case #1314—which one

limbed eight times, ribcaged twice and fed by stroking

          shall neck, jaw, tongue, and teeth? Nose, eyes, don't forget

the fatty joints, abdominal muscles strengthened by names

          electrodes positioned at meridians to trigger soul

massaged into the loved parts prepared for separation.

          must be dry, must be . . . or too much scraping causes

Hold the starved one who refused to wither though

          lost sensation. As she sings, the goal is to soften

nameless, sexless. Why must being require cutting?

          resistance but not prevent a command of movement.

Can't cleave Kwon Young Mee for whom Kim Dongji organized a Pyeongyang birthday feast. Can't cleave Kwon Young Mee teaching the northern orphanage nurse the southern word 입양인. Can't cleave Kwon Young Mee's hands stained with the ash of martyrs who the Americans incinerated inside the hospital's basement. Can't cleave Kwon Young Mee's skepticism, her despair at the southern DMZ's tourist buffets and pastel rollercoasters, her memory of Gaesong cornfields and a bus of Greek tourists. Can't cleave Kwon Young Mee singing "Uri Hana" chorused by Kim Chaek University students. Can't cleave Kwon Young Mee's legs as she paces the conference room, her adoption papers spread across the varnished table. Can't cleave Kwon Young Mee, Omma, as the guides read my documents for a map to find you.

Kumgangsan Resort, Gangwon-do, northern Korea

Post-reunion, after the cameras shut off and the crew retreats to smoke cigarettes, the families split apart. Inside the banquet room, they reassemble north and south to gossip about each other. The southerners rub their gold cross necklaces and grumble about the northerners praising Kim Jong Un for the gift of their meeting. The northerners shake blue jars of bulk vitamins, the size of government cheddar, and speculate if their rich relatives mean to shame them.

A Red Cross worker asks a halmoni sitting alone if she regrets reuniting with her oppa wheeled in on a gurney. His dying wish: To apologize for his capture when as a child he picked scrap metal near the enemy's encampment to sell for food. The halmoni sighs and grimaces. The Red Cross worker flips open his smartphone and offers her the SK-NK translator.

Look again at the livid / form striving to live / without a twin

Fused it's more / vital / more present

than if the sculptor severed one from one / Why does freedom

require a death and a life / to create a self

who will need a story / how her newborn body

was taken apart / fashioned into a she?

Made from loss / she understands the making

tears one body from a host / Her urge to see

that rupture is not a romance but a reckoning with power

that could have discarded / could have / reshaped it

into an it / into a him

He reunited with knives, paper skins

peeled and piled on a confetti countertop,

crushed garlic, bowls of rice and cooked blood,

his omma cleaning casings to stuff a slack coil,

an earthenware jar of spoiled beans

that his omma insisted was his favorite food.

먹어 먹어 his omma poked a fingerful inside his cheek,

and he collapsed on the kitchen floor from the taste

as his adopted body rejected

the fermented paste while another birthed itself

insatiable on his hip. It nubbed into a boil

his omma coaxed open with the choicest beef.

It hardened a mouth. Determined

it leached calcium and drained lymph

while hair patterned its crown. As he watched

the vanished twin return legible and lipped

soon to demand a plate, he plotted

how to reabsorb it before it gained a face.

반 갑 습 니 다

Itaewon, Seoul 2013

An hour into reunion Appa and I match
1-2-3-drink! and I want to sing
the only Korean song I know

from the Sariwon farmers developing
fertilizers 반 갑 습 니 다
and the youth league who hand built

a freeway from Pyeongyang to the sea
반 갑 습 니 다. So when Appa teaches me
the Hanja for our family's name

Advocates of the White Phoenix, I ask him
아빠 노래를 좋아요? and he winks
Let's go. 가자 down the street

past Hamilton Hotel and English-only
signs, down basement steps
to an ajumma's red-lit noraebang.

He rents a room and in the swamp glow
of the video screen, he's svelte,
tall, round-eyed. He punches in a code,

tilts the mic toward his lips, and he's 23
Christmas furloughed from the army
and crooning to a woman

he just met about his fugitive heart.
On the TV, deer promenade
in willow grass as he lets loose

a high vibrato and swoops his left arm
above his head. I'm convinced
when he points to me I'm every woman

he gave himself to with this ballad,
and he's every man I ran away from
grateful I got out intact.

When it's my turn, I don't hold back:
동포 여러분 형재 여러분
Dongpo yeorabun hyeongjae yeorabun

Fellow countrymen, fellow brothers
반 갑 습 니 다. 반 갑 습 니 다.
Bangapseumnida! Bangapseumnida!

Nice to meet you! Nice to meet you!
Nice to meet you. Nice
to meet you. Appa

listens on the couch as I belt out
drought, tar pails, pavement home.
My right fist beats time

against my chest. When I finish,
I wait. He sits and sits. From a telescope
distance he studies me and asks

Where did Sujin learn this song?

Dear 동생 ♡

Thank you for translating my letter to your aunt my 언니. I'm sorry that my writing is difficult to read. I continue studying Korean even though I sound like a baby and make many mistakes. I appreciate your and our family's loving patience.

I hope you can catch the fragrance of this letter. Since reunifying five years ago in Seoul, there is so much I've wanted to say to 언니, but I've been trapped by my mouth repeating the phrases I know best. (Are you hungry? I miss you.) We are always rice, apple, meat, and water. Instead of ghosts, we are two stomachs, two mouths babbling about our digestion.

I'm sorry for this burden of translation. While you're in the army, it won't be possible to help 언니 and me. I watch the news reports of continued Korean War, and I am petrified for your life. You're only 22 and your mother's only son. I pray for peace, for reconciliation, for your return home. Love, 누나

"Cities shall suffer siege and some shall fall,
But man's not taken. What the deep heart means,
Its message of the big, round, childish hand,
Its wonder, its simple lonely cry,
The bloodied envelope addressed to you,
Is history, that wide and mortal pang."

— Stanley Kunitz, "Night Letter"

White Horse

Cutlass-shoed   your hooves uproot

The fallen larkspur   catches in axe wheel spurs

Unstitched   the earth gapes

under your nostril-trumpets   unfurling mane-banner

Your white surrenders to ash smear   the righteous

bit soldered to jaw   A caisson's grill

pushes east through cities   forewarned by dropped posters

to bedchambers   of burning oil pits   for pax unum

Your eyes   gouged by the rider astride your back

fell like charred plums   His lancet

twisted in your socket's night   O missile

hurling toward my city have mercy

and swerve

A House in Nicosia

White curtains flutter as if a childish hand
bats at distance

flicks plaster off
ramshackle walls
papered with a politician's face.

In time's slow fray

he's a target
practice for tower guards

overlooking a football field
of plastic bags, red spray cans. A train's
outline heaves across the bleacher's height.

Down concrete steps
a diaspora
of feral cats congress.

Ribbed with longing
they're the only ones who can cross.

It's all guesswork
smeared in a childish hand

writing that wide and mortal pang
called History

that human cry
forced from home one morning.

Through dust and shadow, I see flashlights
bullhorns, dogs, a crash
of drawers, metal spoons and forks,

a long crawl
space under pine boards
torn up revealing a secret

darkness where no one hid
the money, what's left of the canopy

frame's blue drapes
that her husband pulled back
to make love to her.

Young, they left the balcony doors open.
Boys laughed and kicked a ball past midnight.

Now the mattress straddles a threshold
like tides summoning a raft
tied to the firmament.

Tell me.

If two loves claim this house
to whom does it belong?

A Small Guest

Alan Kurdî (2013-2015)

Seaweed followed the law
        It released you to waves bussing
                your small body

down, down dark currents
        silver minnow tunnel. Your red
                shirt swallowed

the Aegean, billowed
        and swelled, but your shoes stayed on
                By them the sea

knew your refuge dream
        restored you to shore so your father
                Abdullah could find you

a guest of the sea
        Without guests all houses would be a grave
                the poet wrote

making a worm from mist
        a bird from sand. What prayer
                transforms this empty

castle guards watch
        ignorant of the gift to shelter each other?
                Who will help

close, open, close
>your velcro laces for the journey
>>your father dares

for your sake? You a gift
>loved with milk cake and honey. You
>>practice the names

to keep you safe—
>not Mohammed, Jesus. Not Muslim
>>Christian. Hush—

don't bother now
>as tourists gather and multiply your image
>>on their tiny screens

You are not their orphan
>of beach foam, Alan *flag bearer,* watching
>>from the lap of God

Moon Jar

for Shynne Gwang-hyun

As the moon descends into the well

the jar inside the well

it reveals a great

emptiness that is the jar

summoning others who will come

after the fact of the jar

disappears inside the moon

Fox

After torching
my ancestral fields for planting,
I drank makgeolli
while the cinders cracked

and tailed. She crept
along the smoky ridge,
her pelt musk amber.
She was always near

in the char licking her paw
shifting as I watched
her pink tongue fasten shapes
the moonlight cast

on my gray sleeve.
On guard I covered my heart
with my flask. She bared
her blackened teeth.

Birdsong for Ten Thousand Years

Koguryeo tomb murals, northern Korea

The dying queen assembled birds that could talk like men—
      parrots, roosters, cranes, mynahs aiding the lost

merchants, magpies carrying muddy twigs to a fissured
      immortal terrace, kestrels, the white falcon

fearless of invading dogs. To guard against four directions
      she consulted the phoenix, tiger, dragon, tortoise-snake.

Each tethered a cosmic map soaked with a blood tree
      where the three-legged crow lodged his command.

Bride to this sunbird, the queen presided, her eye a moon
      mirror for the constellations. Which bird did she prefer

for a song to establish her kingdom for ten thousand years,
      her final wish a pearl embroidered dragon dress

in which to receive the fairies in the endless blue?

Beetle

after Jose Pacheco

You, like all of us, are what you conceal.
Inside your horned helicopter
you hide and suffer,
infamous in your exile. Prized
for your craft that we try to imitate

in gold and amber,
you survive baiting, outrun and elude us,
your assassins who can't follow into the wall,
veldt of circuitry or Jacob's ladders,
this, your solitary confinement
from which you escaped. Winged and on the run,

you entered illegally, the humblest of eaters
pursued by flashlights searching London flats,
chased into floorboards and dreaming
there to engorge yourself on chicken marrow,
hair of a woman
who forged a compatriot's freedom,
lint and nail clippings,
underground palace of discarded excess.

Poor, you never sought to become a rascal,
thief, or tax evader.
Your mouth hooked and clutched,
to secrete a hardening cloak
as instinct instructed. No ambition
could sustain that artist in you
to fulfill the task for which you were born:
an asylum out of your own body

metamorphosing the worm
who curls in all of us who envy
such rapid success, perfected artifice
that, if an autopsy, would reveal nothing about you
that hasn't been pestered
or riddled by schoolchildren, judges,
barbers who can't betray your anonymity
or inform upon your green card stash.

Programmed by shadows, struck dumb
yet knowing to scuttle a deathblow missing,
you do not fear
that kind of death. You have survived it
as you reported to the benefit gala,
the pearl strung collarbones enchanted by
your poise and sung resurrection.

Born and cradled in a ball of shit,
no longer a trespasser but a guest of honor,
you hum from a scroll
and silence the wait staff who once pitied you
but now mutter
you were always untouchable.

Our mumbler, how you alter the story!
Who can rival you in strategic confusion?
Pest because we can't surpass or kill
or ignore you.
Neither an insect nor bird,
you exist in pure imagination.

Your reputation will last
long after the house is dismantled,
its fixtures stripped and auctioned, its metal
hinges scrapped, bricks sold in a yard
then reused for respectable establishments
where the threat of your possibility
will compel precautions

though you disappear again through a crack
into the darkness with which we wall ourselves
but cannot go. How we hate you for it
and spread rumors of your disease,
though we admire your rage to outlive and,
like you, are what we conceal.

Yi Sang's Room

b. Kim Haegyeong | Seochon, Seoul 1910-33

At this table
I pose as an illiterate draftsman

Tax collectors
commissioned me for an imperial museum
but I design my name

as a false frame
though marked by bureaucrats
as an industrious example

There on rafters of bone
I inscribe an orange
butterfly for the virtuous

wives sickened
by their husbands' semen
pumped to Battleship Island

to motor coal cars
The messages the men carve
I want to go home

Beloved I miss you
into the timbered shafts
shingle my roof against a red sun

and within its blaze I cut
lengths of air
for walls that a solitary prisoner

released from Seodaemun
can dream inside
Here I no longer fear

the tenure committee
who prefers red lacquered bowls
to story loss

or administrators
who nail ordinances to my porch
Motherless my words

may be dismissed as experiments
or disappear
under a courtyard lake

or divide a pillared darkness
into floating rooms
in which monks and poets eat

The bronze latch slips
and leaves blow through the gate
Now it's possible

to speak in earnest of escape
Don't let disaster catch you
immobile and bereft

Failure is also a posture against, against

"자유는 만물의 생명이요 평화는 인생의 행복이다."

— 만해 한용운, <님의 침묵 (沈默)>

"Don't be suspicious of me just because I am far away from you."

— Manhae Han Yong-Un,
The Silence of My Love

Birthmother

Shillim, Wonju 1976

A shack creaks on a cornfield's edge. Plum rain

ruins the laundry line kicking a tantrum.

She bites down on knotted cloths to deliver us

into plate clatter, water spilled on ondol floor,

crusted rags, mineral scent. She bites into a dream

of a ruddered craft turned toward out.

▬▬▬▬▬▬

What is more despised than an unwed girl birthing

an unwanted child named for vengeance—

Sujin *River of Truth Flowing from the North*—

sworn to the mountains, to the trees'

labyrinthine roots, to the white shafts' grasp on rot,

to the bitter flavor between life and life

trussed together twisting to unwind, to undo?

▬▬▬▬▬▬

Homeless, she armed herself with sharp things

seen through a train window. Fence wire

bent into a hook. She strung up an idea—

we were dead anyway, lost

outside propriety. This kind of law makes women mean

what they say with their side-eye

silent treatment learned from mothers who

kept their distance. She practiced above her stomach, my head

knocking on the pelvic door locked tight.

———

She couldn't do it though she wanted to cut

and run. The noon heat intervened trailing

a cawl across my face sticky, strawberry-

bruised. She said cousin Sunil convinced her

I was beautiful though ravenous, rooting.

She knew I'd locate her. Someone else had to slice me

free from watermelon rinds, silk husks boiled for tea

to trick the stomach twitching while selling summer corn

roadside en route to the city. No matter how far

she turned facing the wall to forget, I followed.

I threw myself at her when hands dragged me up, away.

Note Left at a U.S. Camptown Brothel for My Missing Imo

Dear Sixth Imo, Grandfather's youngest daughter,

No one taught you to write "petal" / unfurling red across the bed /

creek cutting the mattress / No one told me your name / chalk to

sketch your body starred and open / so Grandmother could buy rice

while the neighbors ate barley / Nobody asked where her money came

from / They knew where youngest daughters disappeared to / why

their mixed babies disappeared too / what math purchased seaweed

for soup fed to the married eldest delivering a son / The first time I

heard the rumor of you it was a mistake / to ask your name because

Omma wanted to hide you / Just as she hid the fact of me I also hid

the words I knew—kijichon, yanggongju, koa, ibyeongah / I hid under

the bed, in the cupboard, behind clay pots / all the names for absence

feeding our family who chewed and chewed

Orphan Rescue

Yongsan U.S. Army Garrison, Seoul | for David

While your mother's dicing spam and canned wieners in the canteen, you're in the company of soldiers who've named you "Scoot" because you sit on a swivel chair, test-driving across the mess hall by your heels. You're twelve. Your mother makes sure you're clean. The soldiers laugh anyway at the army surplus shirt's gaping neckline as you lean forward focusing your body's force, your skinny arms pumping to slingshot. You're not going anywhere. You don't know how. So an E-2 private from Arkansas does what his shy pals are thinking of. He grabs the metal back and spins you round and round, and you're wide-mouthed surprised, wind hitting the back of your throat. You hear the thud of your mother's cleaver against the countertop, bubbling red broth, her groaning aigoo while the Jamisul poster girl's heart-shaped face blurs into a stars-and-striped banner for Company Charlie Twelve: *We serve the burn.* You don't want rescue as the private swerves you from wall to wall until you fall through a hole of soldiers encircling you, taking turns for a spin: *Am I your father? Am I your father? Am I your father? Am I your father? Am I your father?* Their faces streak into light so you can't discern, can't stop the giggling centrifuge or the sour welling in your belly, or hail your mother still sighing while she stirs the base camp stew.

Red Baiting

after Carol Muske-Dukes

You've ruined my daughter's bat mitzvah!
So what if she's adopted from Guangzhou? How dare you

speak altering our story when its ours. How dare you
speak at all. *Bitch, we're warning you*

you're nothing to this editorial committee
but a schemer lock stepping north to a red star.

We've rung the vine and cc:ed K so she knows
the Seoul expats blacklisted you. They're watching

our blog's social feed. Unreliable you write lies.
Even your best metaphors stick

like rusted toasters trap bread for flies. Why do you
blow more hot air than a Thanksgiving parade's

mylar penguins untethered from their handlers,
their gravitas rises above skyscrapers,

their egos wheeze from one hemisphere to another
and knock out weather station transmitters?

Why must you always get in our way? We're sorry
you're angry because you had a bad childhood

that you peddle as another rhyme
no one will read. We're telling you this

because you need to heal. Nobody likes you
though no one will tell you, and people around here talk.

How to Eat Your Love

우리 엄아 애게 | for Omma

In your version, I come back deformed / a ghost, turned backward

bare feet, decayed teeth / raiding our ancestors' tombs, meat stripped

mouse bones thrown at your door. / So you bow your head

stud the boiling red with white knuckles / of young radish as I lick

the lock unable to cross / a rope of chili peppers announcing

your son's birth. The eldest I was a secret / vessel of your rage—

all digestion, I clenched and uncoiled across your pelvis

seizing the greasy bits / you scraped

portioned by the textile factory's canteen. The machines

cranked and thrust. Spitting they fingered every orifice

looped into fresh skein a dark thread / you cursed. *If only it would slide out*

For whom do I interpret this fury? *Forgive me,* you say

I was poor, alone / In the economic miracle we were all raw

material, orphaned to fetch / hard currency

like Jeolla-do girls groomed for kisaeng tours, now birth

mothers to the missing crated overseas to military allies

The North reports of a child sold to a New York circus

Let me see my father, Kim Il Sung! she pleads

from the cage / of hook-nosed American greed. I don't believe that

my colleague Cho translated the adopted boy

calling 아저씨, 도와주세요 / *Uncle, help me go home!*

to the white parents carrying him into the Texas Denny's

Eat to remember / to forget each other eat

the charred flesh / lettuce parcels / of conscripted uncles

night-delivered from Vietnam, shrouded in flags / Open your mouth

to the unreliable ones hidden in Russian snow, camptown princesses

"dust of the streets" mixed and nameless / they searched

restaurant scraps as kin to you / a farm girl squatting

to push out contaminants making you sick

Clogged toilet shared by eight families / slabbed on the dorm floor

All that waste / the factory churned into the river

somehow cleaned blood out of your best cotton dress

Your image struts on stage / righteous and full as

S performs a defector eating rice / evening KBS / nuclear threat

absorbed as nutrients / Her body radiates like a transmitter

slogans I heard in Pyeongyang / a parked truck blaring unity songs

during morning rush hour / She eats with precision the ghosts

of her amputation / A scripted regime / collapse produces bodies

mute, grim, consuming / shades / where the missing

limbs can still be felt / Here, Omma, you claim a summons

to build your prayer house / The fourth wall falls away

Platters of grilled pork, three fish picked apart later / you beat

my shoulders casting out histories locked in the muscle / You entreat

a scar-eyed Jesus to restore my barren womb / You design my resurrection

like the military engineers personhood

through syllabi and "great books" / star students

trained in singing / A veteran, the professor reminisced about the head

he buried miles from the Korean soldier's body / Well-intentioned

he ate a cookie while the class studied his photos / I'm supposed to chew

the dead / again and again in effigy / You order me to

go to church to atone for your sins / to forget

because we're "a well-fed nation" / He wrote to the administration

proud of his service, furious at his censure / casting me

out as a woman he could've bought in a camptown / all the children

he rescued with chocolate and socks / a bitter orphan who

the generalissimo outfitted with explosives

Untenurable / with slim fingers I could wire a shrapnel storm

You revise me into a functional body / you stuff with duck meat

expensive fruits and kim—bribes so I'll translate your way home

to your baby son / I tire of use but here's my left hand rewriting

this DMZ gorge and purge economy / Who can begrudge you

a 빨리빨리 mise en scène? / So my illiterate brother will remember

you pack suitcases of mountain roots / I'll cook as your surrogate

With each bite his limbs retract into a toddler kidnapped, sent away

now craving / And I ring with cartilage 반환하는 혼이

a ghost pink and fattening inside my belly / You at last

free from history / O sticky hunger

cut down from the rafters of my dry breasts / New person eating

two into one / You discard the extraneous

girl / hide and scoop up the boy

Korean Heritage House

Saint Paul, Minnesota 2015 | for Brooke Newmaster

A dress rack of hanbok press against a row of drums mounted in rainbow wooden frames. Metal shelves heave with folk games, pink feather-edged fans for a dance troupe, wooden masks, Shilla court wigs, boxes of calendars, hanji paper lotus flowers, banchan bowls, plastic colanders, a rice cooker so large you could bathe a baby inside or feed forty families lunch. It has. You can lose your keys and coat to KSL workbooks dog-eared and underlined, ink-caked calligraphy brushes, handled air-lock boxes stuffed with pickled cucumber and perilla leaves all stacked wherever there's space because here it's 어서 오세요! Welcome hunger! Welcome loss! Here's the corner kitchen where two ajummas who don't know their Korean mothers (One searched; one didn't.) stuff kimbap with marinated tofu from Kim's Oriental down the street, a wall of mirrors that three boys will ignore as they concentrate on striking janggo drums 1, 2, 3 while their father types a message into Google translate to email his omma in Daegu. In the conference room, there's a corner pyramid of empty gallon jars from a kimchi-eating contest to raise funds for unwed moms in Seoul. In the bathroom, there's new dry wall that took two guys an afternoon to install over the hole some thieves jackhammered trying to tunnel to the Hmong jeweler next door. (They gave up after an inch into concrete.) There's a widescreen plasma TV someone donated. A broken copy machine. Inside the fridge, somebody left ddakjook made from two boxes of leftover Popeye's fried chicken, and a Facebook post announces it's there for whomever wants to scoop some out. There are ziplock bags in the far left drawer next to the chopsticks drawer. Go and help yourself.

The Telling

"We were anxiously waiting for Koreans from the north. And just over the crest of the horizon, a light glowed. It was a group of people holding candles wading down the river."

—Christine Ahn

In your dream, the fathers come from four directions

gowned in dawn. They carry the broken

sons from the grassy banks and descend

to submerge waist high in the center where the law

cannot force them to forget or to remember

the joy of the cool water, how the riverbed

pillows their scabbed feet, the pleasure of belonging

to no nation. They congregate as one

peace made from the male parts

disarmed and unarmored, and as the currents wash over

their tenderest flesh shocked by the gentle sway, as a softening

wells inside their groins and chests, they surrender

to how good it feels to surrender.

And you depart upriver, a Korean woman testing the surreal

death worlds others invent about our northern relatives

whom they've never met, or who infiltrate the north disguised

as teachers weaponizing their gifts to smuggle out the true

story that is always the same story

clicking shut inside an unceasing war

horse thrashed into a blind courier.

But you, who can see and hear, attend to the dream

that shows its hands, that fragile moment between

you and Park Dongji. *We want to be seen as human.*

Tell them we are human, she said. Tell them the dream

of the grandmother who stirs a brass pot over campfire

and ladles a dark substance into the children's pails

to carry over a mountain. Tell them the women of many nations

quilted cloth from many nations in Gaesong. Tell of their song

We are one. We are one. Tell them she,

whose hands shrapnel severed, steadied the bright fabric

as the women sewed even though South Koreans phoned in

threats of arrest and acid thrown on the women's faces

if they crossed the DMZ

of the southerners' imaginations. Tell them

there is only the telling that can create a home

no matter how unseen or preposterous

that originates as a murky sludge, an elemental soup

on the tongue and cared for over a hearth

that could nourish us again

if we tell ourselves, sister and brother,

together we want to live.

Acknowledgments

My gratitude to the editors of *Agni, Asian American Literary Review, Blackbird, Columbia: A Journal of Art and Literature, Diode Poetry Journal, Dublin Review, Freshwater Review, Fulcrum, Indiana Review, Journal of the Motherhood Initiative, Jubilat, Levure Littéraire, Marsh Hawk Review, MIRAMAR, Solo Novo, TRUCK,* and *Words Without Borders* for publishing some of the poems contained in this collection, some of which appear here in slightly revised forms. Thank you to the anthologists who collected my work for *2012 Seoul International Writers Festival, Azaleas: an Anthology of Korean and Korean American Women's Poetry, Borderlands & Crossroads: Writing the Motherland, Nothing to Declare: A Guide to the Flash Sequence,* and *One for the Money: The Sentence as a Poetic Form.*

A version of "Notes from a Missing Person" first appeared as "Fetish Mothers" in my digital mixed-media chapbook titled *Notes from a Missing Person* (Laramie: Essay Press, 2015). I am grateful to the editors Andy Finch and Christiana Baik.

I deeply appreciate the organizers of Art Song Lab, the International Writing Program's New Symposium in Paros, Korean Education and Exposure Program-DPRK, Korean Friendship Association, Korean Unwed Mothers and Families Association, and Nodutdol for Korean Community Development for facilitating invaluable experiences that sharpened my imagination.

Grants from He-Shan World Fund of the Tides Foundation, Intermedia Arts, Korea Policy Institute, Korean Unwed Mothers Support Network, Minnesota State Arts Board, and St. Olaf College assisted me with the research and writing of this book.

I am blessed by a powerful transnational community of artists, poets, and intellectuals in particular Kristin Naca, Jane Jin Kaisen, Gus Sondin-Kung, Lisa Lewis, Dinah Cox, Aimee Parkison, Bert and Sarah

Ballard, Kit Myers, Shannon Gibney, Moe Lionel, Sherry Fernandez-Williams, Jenny Wills, Mads Them Nielsen, David Mura, Stevie Larson, SooJin Pate, Caitlin Kee, Kurt Blomberg, Juyeon Rhee, Hélène Cardona, Joan Hepburn, Jonathan Naito, Linda Mokdad, and Cleo Granneman whose generosities aided this book's completion.

My enduring thanks to Dennis Maloney and Elaine LaMattina at White Pine Press for a literary homeland and to Carol Muske-Dukes, Christopher Merrill, and Viet Thanh Nguyen for lighting this book's entrance into the world.

Thank you to my husband Dr. Stefan Liess and to our son Thomas. Thank you to my brother Lee Jae Hoon and to his sons/my choka Jordan, Ian, and Corey. Thank you to my sister Holly Pasmore and to my brother's family who have welcomed me with generosity and kindness.

Always to my relations in northern and southern Korea whose names cannot be written here because of the continued repression of imaginations like mine that refuse to accept unending Korean War. 사랑하고기억해요. 우리는 꿈에서 여기에서 만고 이인생에서 다시 만날 것입니다. I love and remember you. We meet here in a dream, and we will meet again in this life.

Notes

The images, punctuating this collection, are in order of appearance:

Retake: Mayday. 3-channel video installation, Jane Jin Kaisen, 2011. This still image from Kaisen's *Retake: Mayday* is sourced from *Mayday on Cheju-do*, a 1948 archive film held in the U.S. National Archives.

Reproduction of "미군기지촌1965년 (American Camp-town 1965)," xerox copy of Shisei Kuwabara, 격동한국50년 (Seoul: Noonbit, 2015).

"Orphan Hojuk," carbon copy on paper, from the author's personal collection.

"Uri Omma Eggae," black ink on 8.5 x 11 white paper, by the author, 2016.

Google Maps street view screenshot of Snelling Avenue between Van Buren and Blair Avenues in Saint Paul, Minnesota, United States.

Dorason May 24, 2015. Digital C-print,, Jane Jin Kaisen, 2015. The photograph depicts camera flashes from a large crowd of waiting journalists when Kaisen, as part of a women's delegation, crossed the DMZ from northern Korea into southern Korea on May 24th, 2015.

"I confess I traveled"
Just months before the Jeju 4.3 Incident, the newly formed Republic of Korea enacted the 국가안보법 or National Security Law (NSL) effectively criminalizing exchange and communication between North

and South Korea as anti-state activities. Historically, international human rights activists and the U.S. State Department have denounced South Korea's broad application of the NSL to repress democratic organizing and free speech. The epigraphs opening this book excerpt from the Democratic Lawyers Association's English translation available at http://antinsl.jinbo.net/nsl_full_text_en.html.

Under South Korean president Park Geunhye's administration, there has been a dramatic uptick in the number of adjudicated NSL cases including the 2015 indictment of Korean American author Shin Eun Mi whose "alleged offense was to describe conditions in North Korea in a positive manner, although she also criticized conditions" (*Human Rights Watch*). See Choe Sang-Hun, *New York Times* "South Korea Deports American Over Warm Words about North Korea" 10 January 2015 available at:

http://www.nytimes.com/2015/01/11/world/asia/south-korea-to-deport-american-over-warm-words-about-north-korea.html.

"Take young men as coal miners"
For an account of Battleship Island's history as a forced labor camp during Japan's colonization of Korea, see
https://www.theguardian.com/world/2015/jul/03/battleship-island-a-symbol-of-japans-progress-or-reminder-of-its-dark-history.

"The Origins Inside Kim Dae Shik"
See 친일인명사전, vol. 1 (민족문제연구소: Seoul, 2009) 290 for an account of Kim Dae Shik's crimes as a 친일파 (Japanese collaborator) and his role as a former president of Holt Adoption Agency. In a preliminary 2008 list published in *Oh My News*, , founding president of the Eastern Social Welfare Society Kim Duk Whang (김득황 金得榥) is listed as a Japanese collaborator for his activities in Manchukuo. Although his name does not appear in the final edition of 친일인명사전, it was not cleared of culpability due to a lack of

definitive evidence. See
http://www.ohmynews.com/NWS_Web/view/at_pg.aspx?CNTN_
CD=A0000889220 and https://ko.wikipedia.org/wiki/민족문제
연구소의_친일인명사전_수록자_명단_-_해외.

"A Forest in Jeju, Southern Korea"
This poem is triggered by stills from Jane Jin Kaisen's 3-channel video installation *Retake: Mayday* (2011) based on the propaganda film "May Day on Cheju-do" (1948) produced by the United States Military in Jeju Island, South Korea. Kaisen writes in a curatorial statement:

> Being one of the only existing moving images shot in Jeju at the time, *Mayday on Cheju-do* has become a principal visual record of the Jeju April Third Incident, one of the largest and most brutal massacres in 20th century Korean history. The film, which presents itself as documentary truth, was made to show how alleged communists committed arson in Ora Village in Jeju. In actuality, the village was burned down by the US military as part of the film production and at a closer look, it becomes apparent that the film includes various staged and fabricated scenes with actors.
>
> In actuality, the vast majority of casualties during the Jeju April Third Incident were committed onto civilians by state authorities, along with paramilitary groups, under supreme command of the U.S. military government in Korea.

"Northern Korea Postcard: Panmunjom, DMZ"
I paraphrase lines from Kim So Wol's poem "Azaleas (진달래꽃)."
Kim So Wol, *Azaleas: A Book of Poems*, trans. David R. McCann. (New York: Columbia University Press, 2007) 153.

"Reading Keith Wilson's 'The Girl'"
See Keith Wilson, *Graves Registry* (Livingston: Clark City Press, 1972) 21

and and critic William D. Ehrhart, "The Dirty and Murderous Joke: The Korean War Poetry of Keith Wilson," *Revistas de Estudios Norteamericanos* 2003, 9: 39-64.

"Notes on from a Missing Person"
References to Cheng, Jameson via Crapanzano, Koo, and Meyers are drawn from:

> Cheng, Vincent. *Inauthentic: The Anxiety Over Culture and Identity.* New Brunswick: Rutgers UP, 2004.
>
> Crapanzano, Vincent. "The Postmodern Crisis: Discourse, Parody, Memory." *Rereading Cultural Anthropology.* Ed. George E. Marcus. Raleigh-Durham: Duke UP, 2000. 87-102.
>
> Koo, Hagen. *Korean Workers: The Culture and Politics of Class Formation.* Ithaca: Cornell UP, 2001.
>
> Myers, Kit. "Love and Violence in Transracial/national Adoption." American Studies Association Annual Meeting, November 2009, Washington D.C.

I also refer to my research in "Real Support for Unwed Moms" 30 October 2009 in *The Korea Times*:
http://www.koreatimes.co.kr/www/news/opinon/2011/02/198_5457 5.html.

"Parasitic Twin"
See Dana Weiser's "Parasitic Twin" 2008-09. Stoneware, clay, paint, and lacquer, 31 X 12 X 3. *Tending the Speculative: Poems from the Asian American Adoptee Diaspora* , 5 July 2013
http://aaww.org/tending-the-speculative/5/.

"White Horse"
A verse from John of Patmos motivates this poem: "Suddenly, I saw heaven open, and there was a white horse" (Revelation 19:11).

"A House in Nicosia"
This poem is for Neshe Yashin and her poem "My Country Is Cut in Two." In 1974, Turkey invaded Cyrpus, and a demilitarized zone (commonly referred to as The Green Line) was established running the width of the island nation through its capital Nicosia. Reunification talks continue at the time of this book's publication. Many thanks to David St. John, Christopher Merrill, Nataša Durovicová, Debra Marquart, Natasha Tretheway, Stephanos Stephanides, and Anastassis Vistonitis for their friendship and support during my participation in the International Writing Program's Paros New Symposium, which enabled the writing of this poem.

I allude to a line from Stanley Kunitz's poem "Night Letter" from which I also quote for a book section's epigraph. See Stanley Kunitz, *The Collected Poems* (New York: W.W. Norton, 2002) 60-61.

"A Small Guest"
See Khalil Gibran's poem "Sand and Foam," the source text for my allusion to "making a worm from mist." As a participant in Art Song Lab 2016, I completed an earlier version of this poem titled "Song for a Small Guest" for composer Nebal Maysaud. Thank you to pianist Corey Hamm and tenor Will George for the art song's powerful debut at the Roundhouse in Vancouver, Canada and to Art Song Lab's co-directors Alison d'Amato, Ray Hsu, and Michael Park.

My gratitude to Alan's aunt Tima Kurdî for her feedback on the art song version of this poem and her request that we commit our support to the living.

"Moon Jar"
This poem is based on a rare moon jar exhibited at Leeum, Samsung Museum of Art in Seoul. My thanks to Professor Shynne Gwang-hyun for guiding me to this image.

"Birdsong for Ten Thousand Years"
Designated as a UNESCO world heritage site, the Koguryeo tomb murals located in Pyeongyang and surrounding provinces in northern Korea inspire this poem. In Koguryeo cosmology, there were five directions: north, south, east, west, and the center. Of these, the center was the most powerful. It appeared as a sun and inside a samjoko, or three-legged crow, dwelled.

"Yi Sang's Room"
Born Kim Hae-gyeong and adopted by his uncle, the great modernist poet changed his name to Yi Sang after a Japanese survivor mistakenly called him Mr. Lee. According to critic David McCann, this sobriquet "[marked] his notice of, resistance against, and existence within Japanese occupation." The poet lived in Seochon in Seoul, and although his original home no longer exists, a hanok built on the same land was renovated in 2012 and opened to the public. *The Joongang Daily* reported that Yi Sang lived and wrote in "a small dark room" and had no concept of a house. In my poem, I briefly quote from his seminal work *The Wings.* (Seoul: Jimoondang, 2001).

"How to Eat Your Love"
I refer to Theater Mu's 2016 production of Mia Chung's *You for Me for You* performed at the Guthrie in Minneapolis. Thank you to Theater Mu's artistic director Randy Reyes and to KEEP-DPRK alumnus Kurt Blomberg.

"Korean Heritage House"
Originally located on Snelling Avenue, this cultural community space closed and then reopened inside Sejong Academy, a Korean immersion school, in 2015. Its founder and director is Brooke Jee-In Newmaster who also leads the Jang-mi Korean Dance and Drum group.

"The Telling"
In May 2015, Christine Ahn organized "Women Cross the DMZ" and

led thirty international women to Pyeongyang to journey together to Seoul in the name of peaceful reunification. Ahn is co-founder of the Korea Policy Institute and a contributor to *The New York Times/International Herald Tribune, CNN, Asia Times,* and the *San Francisco Chronicle.* I dedicate this poem to her in gratitude for her work and vision. Christine Ahn, "Why Women Must End the Korean War," 8 March 2013, *Foreign Policy in Focus:*

http://fpif.org/why_women_must_end_the_korean_war/.

Jennifer Kwon Dobbs is the author of *Paper Pavilion* (White Pine Press Poetry Prize 2007), *Interrogation Room* (White Pine Press 2018), and the chapbooks *Notes from a Missing Person* (Essay Press 2015) and the German-translated *Necro Citizens* (hochroth Verlag). A recipient of grants from the Daesan Foundation, Minnesota State Arts Board among others, she is associate professor of creative writing and program director of Race and Ethnic Studies at St. Olaf College. She lives in Saint Paul, Minnesota.

Author's photograph by Thaiphy Phan-Quang.